50 Beautiful Birds From Around The World

Adult Coloring Book for Stress Relief and Relaxation

Hello Bird Lovers!

This is the **50 Beautiful Birds From Around the World Adult** Coloring Book. Thank you for your purchase. I sincerely appreciate it. We all know that **coloring** helps to chill us out, so go ahead and be creative and draw to your heart's content!

Inside this **50 Beautiful Birds From Around the World** Coloring book, you'll find: 50

BEAUTIFUL COLORING PAGES

PLUS 50 BLANK PAGES TO GET EVEN MORE CREATIVE 8X11
SINGLE SIDED PAGES
50 UNIQUE PATTENS AND DESIGNS
OVER 100 PAGES OF FUN, INDULGING AND HUMOROUS PATTER**NS FOR**
RELAXATION

If you find this book helpful, would you please be so kind and take a minute to leave us a positive review.

Once again, thank you so much. Please be sure to check out our other coloring books.

- The Ultimate Weed Coloring Book – 50 Amazing Marijuana and Cannabis Themed Images for Relaxation and Stress Relief for Your Mind and Body

- Fucking Awesome Marijuana Themed Coloring Book for Adults – Unique Cannabis Designs with Weed Words for Stress Relief and Relaxation

- **Fucking Awesome Marijuana Themed Coloring Book for Adults – Cannabis Mandalas with Weed Words for Stress Relief and Relaxation**

This book is copyrighted with the Epic Media Publishing Company. Please do not distribute any uncolored pages to anyone in any form including uploading it on social media or any other website.

You can also scan and print the images for personal use, and color them as many times as you like on different types of paper.

Happy Coloring!

This Book Belongs to:

....

Duck

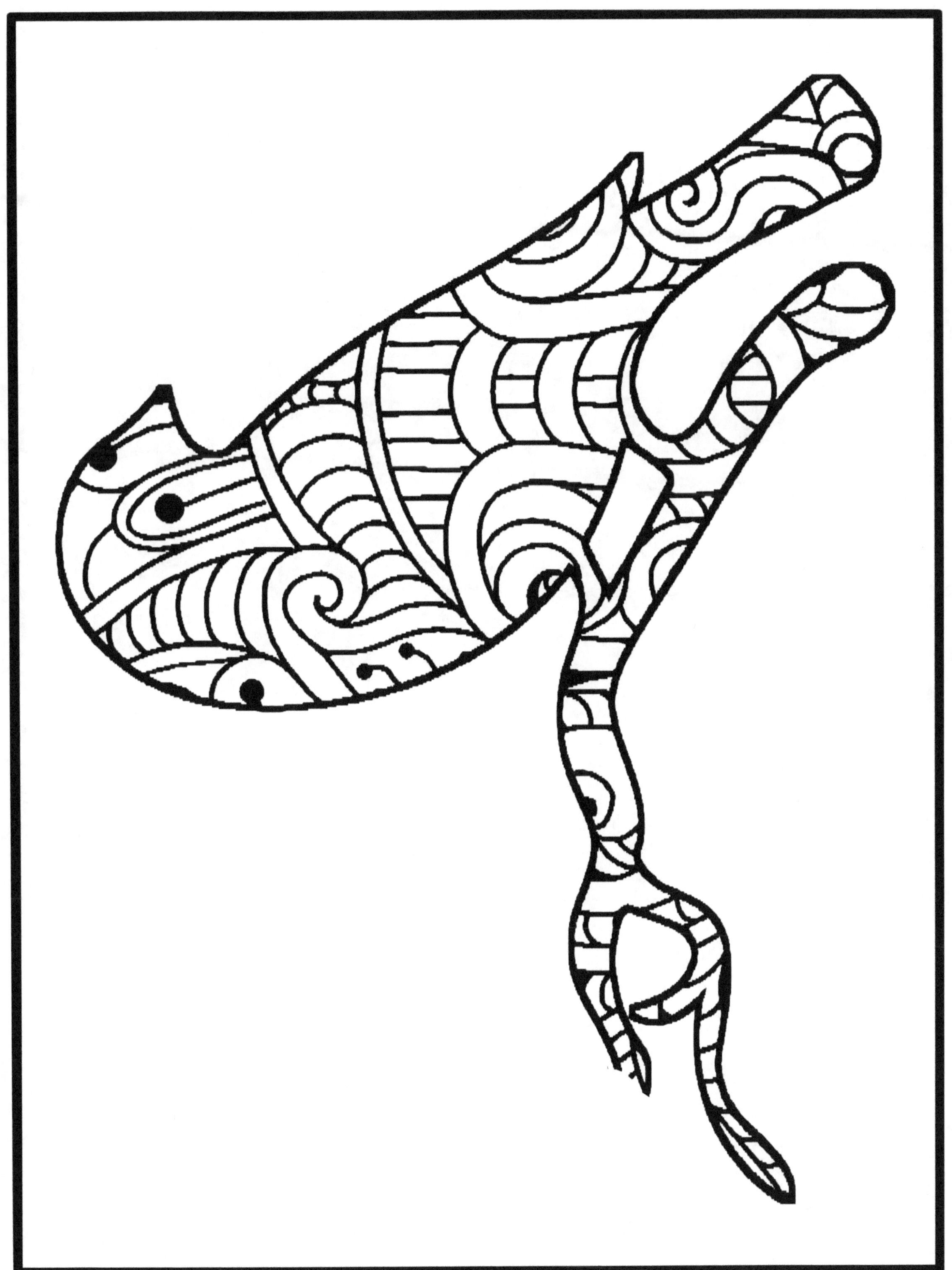

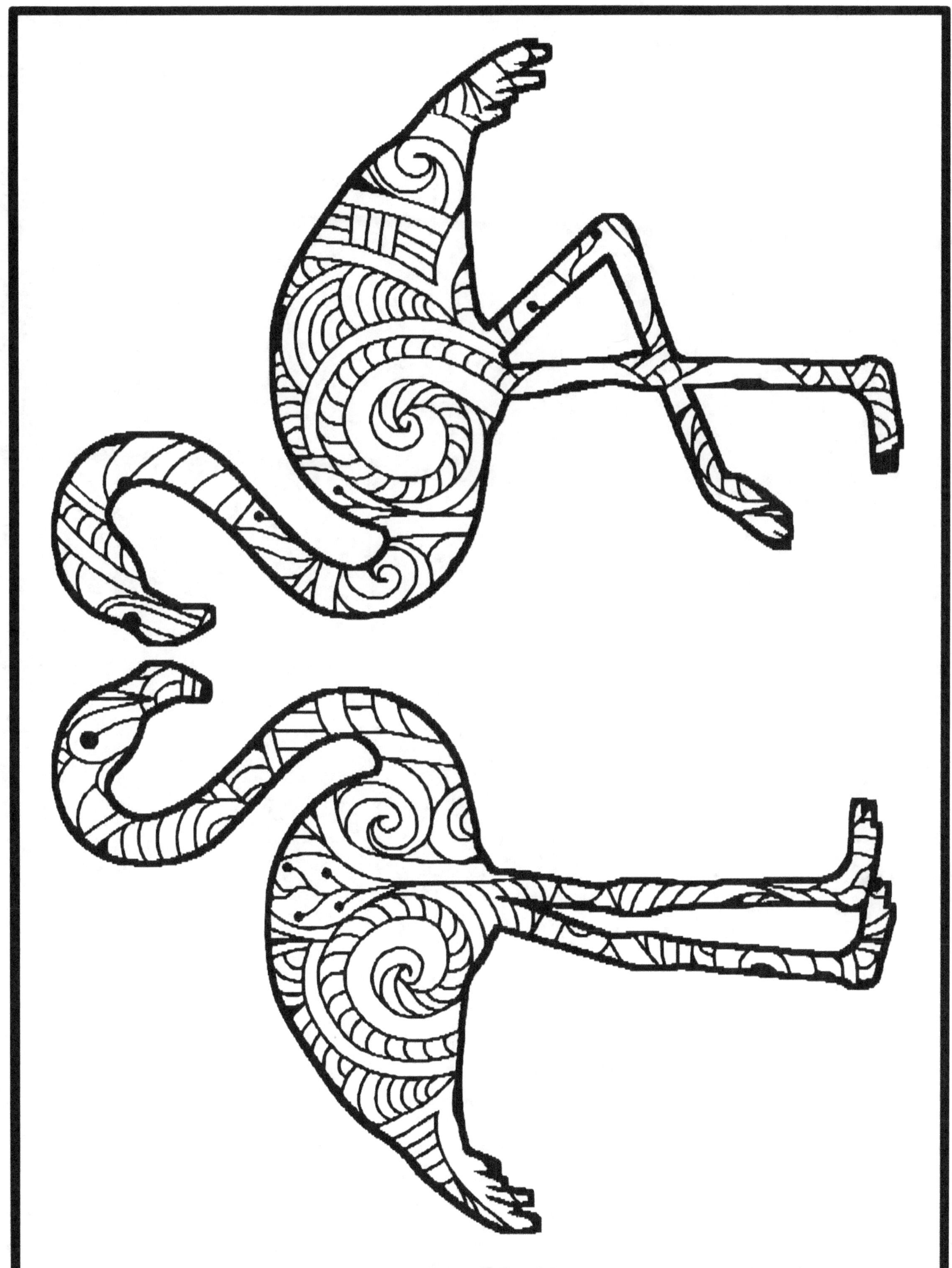

Duck

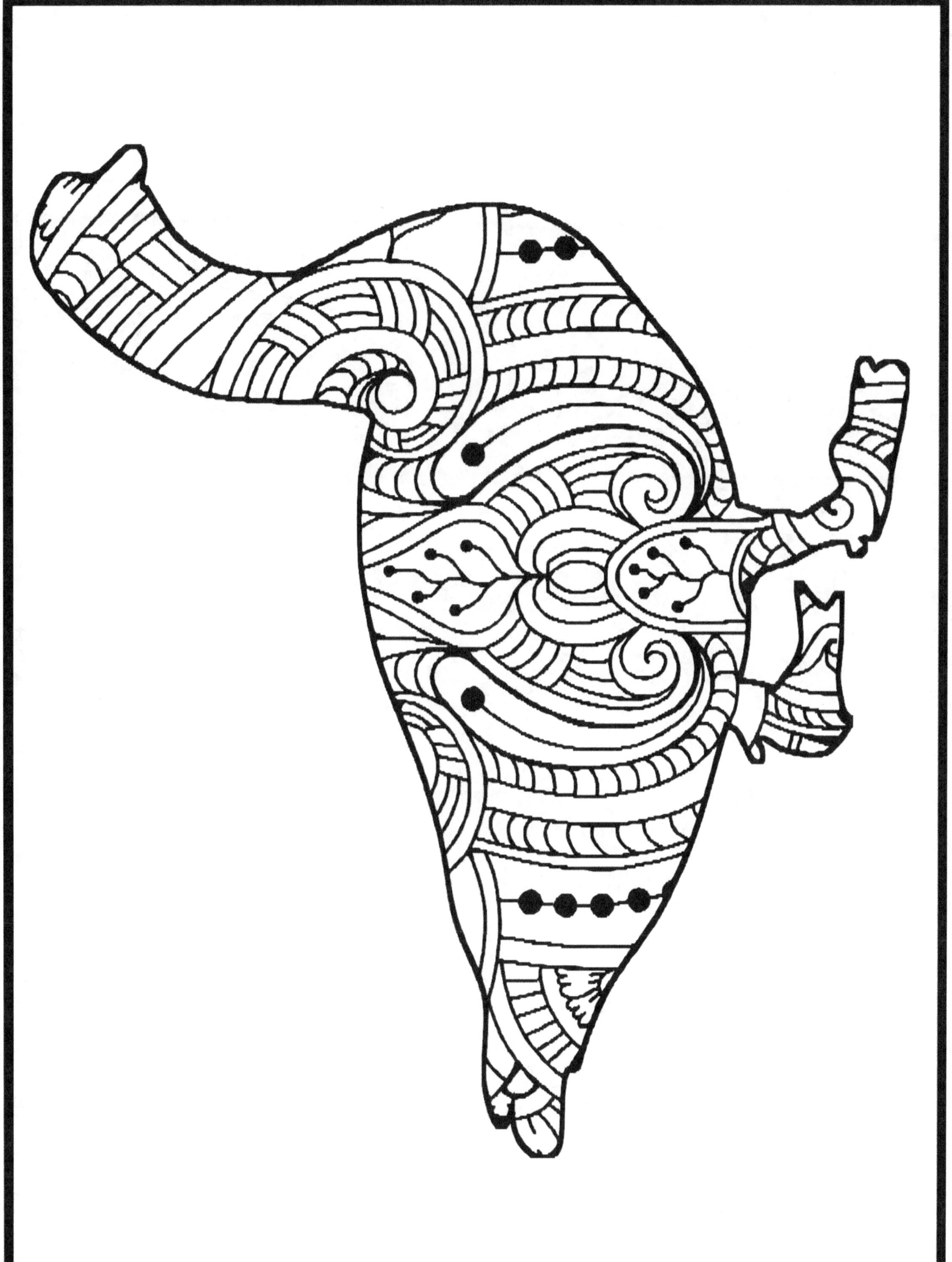

Eagles
vs

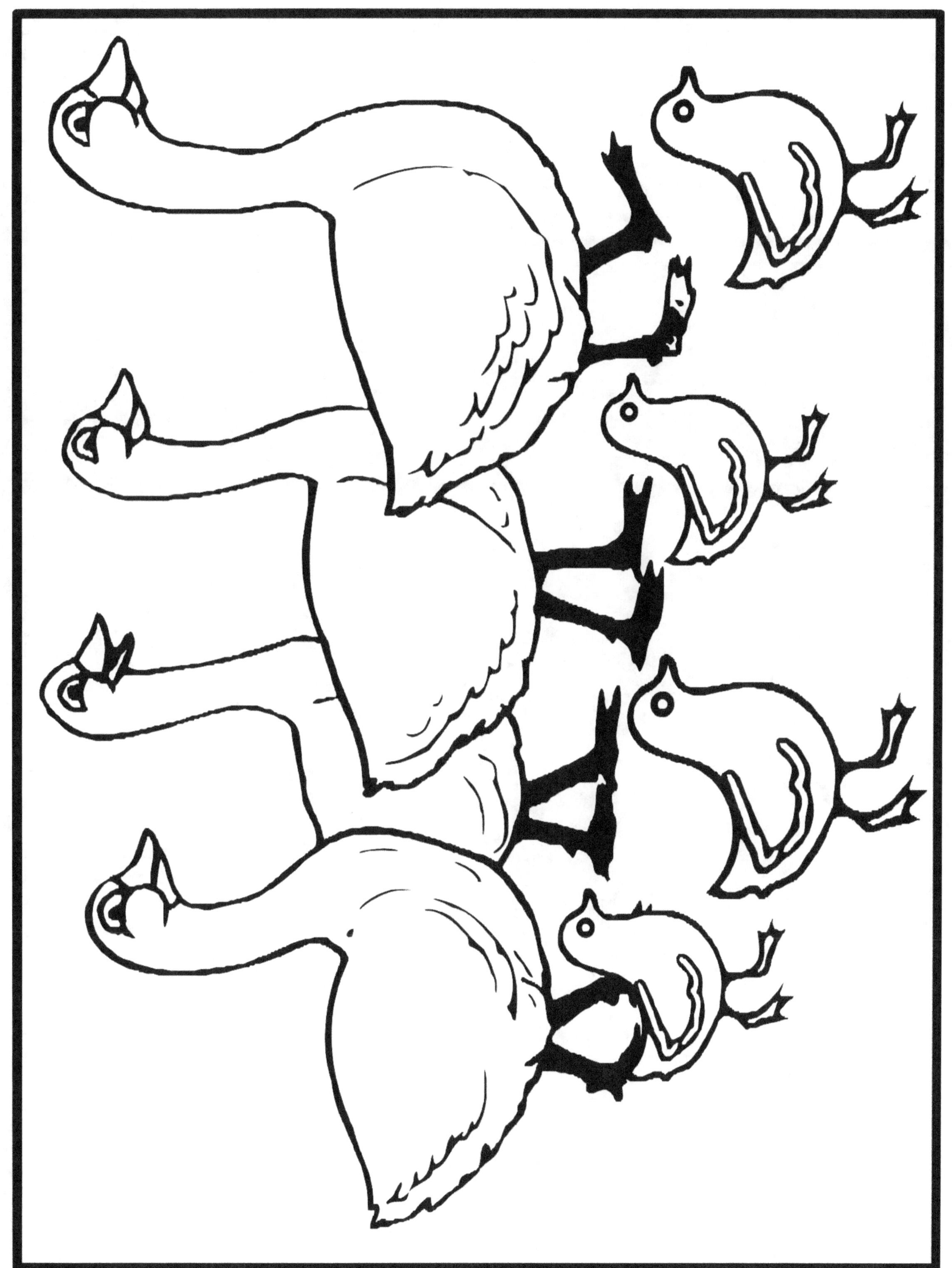

Eagle

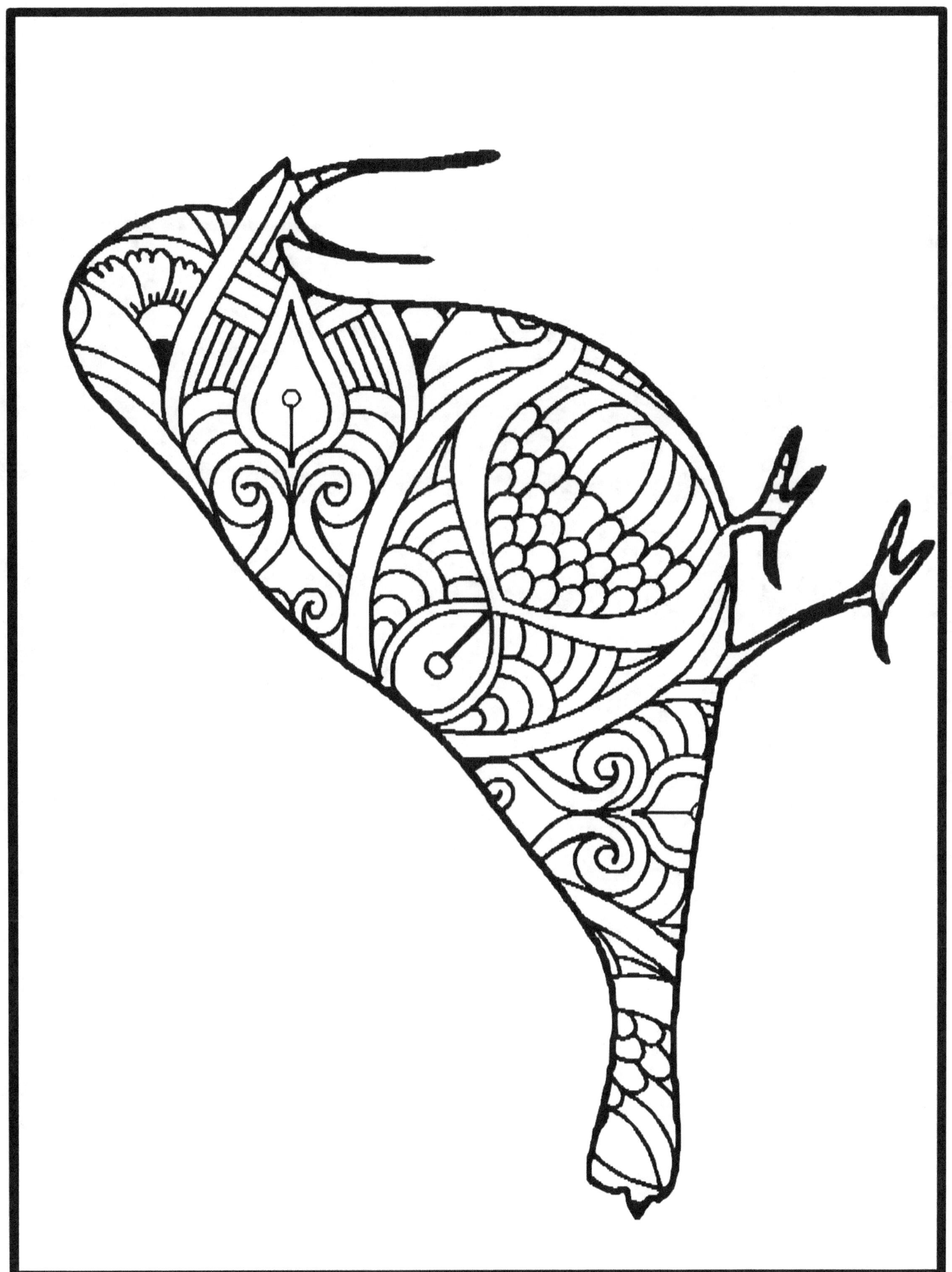